casals

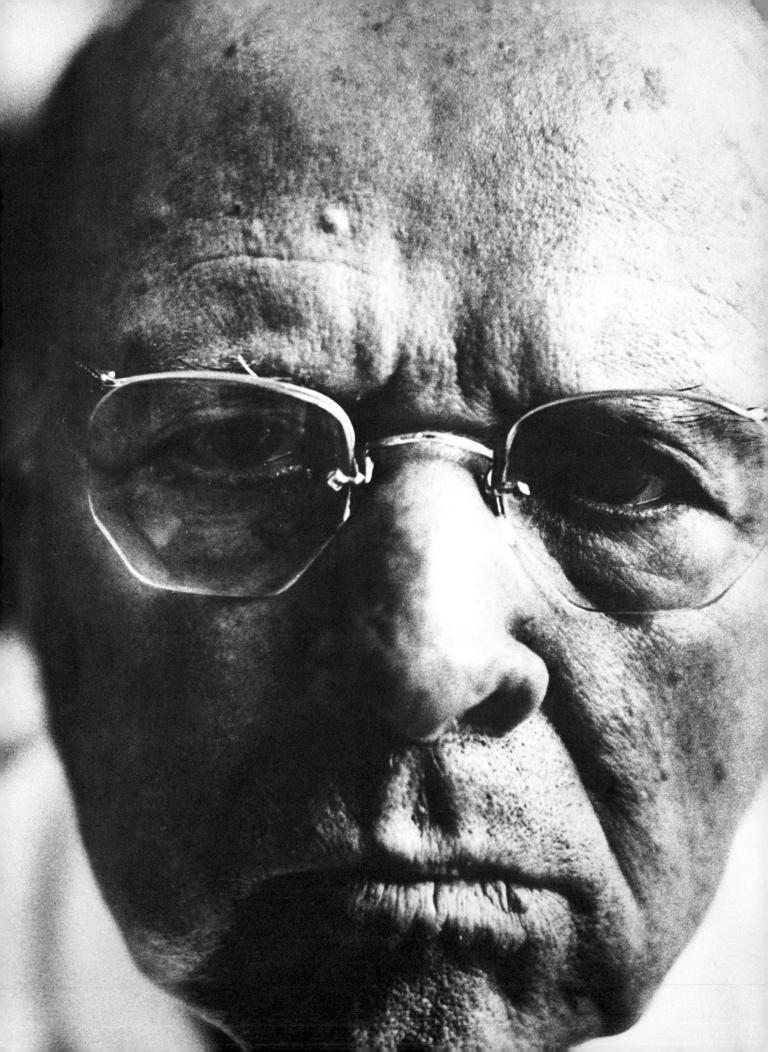

casals

Photographed by Vytas Valaitis

Text selected and arranged by Theodore Strongin

PARAGRAPHIC BOOKS
A DIVISION OF GROSSMAN PUBLISHERS
NEW YORK

Vytas's wish was to dedicate his book to Casals, the man he most admired. He did not live to see his work completed, but his wish is now fulfilled.
—Vanda Valaitis

A NOTE ABOUT THE PHOTOGRAPHER
Lithuanian born, Vytas Valaitis came to the United States after World War II. He received his B.A. in photography from Ohio University in 1959. Vytas was a member of the photographic staff of *Newsweek* for four years and then became a free-lancer. A father of three daughters, he met his untimely death in a scooter accident in October, 1965.

ACKNOWLEDGMENTS

The publishers wish to thank Arnold Steinhardt, Michael Tree, John Dalley and David Soyer, all members of the Guarneri String Quartet, who spent a good deal of time looking at Vytas Valaitis's photographs and discussing them with the editor. All the musicians' quotes in the book are from these men. Thanks, too, to Edward Schreiber, for the use of tapes and soundtracks of his Academy Award-winning film, *Casals Conducts,* and to Alan Rich for the use of his Pacifica Foundation tapes of the Casals master classes in Berkeley, California. Equally, the publishers are grateful to Mr. Jack Delano, for the use of the soundtrack from the film *Pablo Casals en Puerto Rico.*

INTRODUCTION

*P*ablo Casals' most characteristic expressions—his sounds—are not in this, or any, book.

His cello sounds are easy to find on recordings. But when he conducts in rehearsal (sometimes even in concert) or teaches a master class, he has an overwhelmingly typical way of singing to illustrate what he means. These singing sounds are as representative of him and have as much of a personal stamp as his cello playing. They are not as often heard in public. Practically any musician who has worked with him, when asked about his conducting or teaching, bursts into an imitation of Casals' singing—a fantastically complex combination of melodious glides, booming grunts, melting swoops, shattering sputters, all completely unified and completely centered on his musical target, the phrase. They are impossible to render in print. It has been tried. They are the nearest thing to cello possible with the human voice.

"Laeei–laeei–aiee–dugadaeei . . . laeei–duga-dugadaeei"—all originating deep in the diaphragm and with the complete constellation of emphases, of retards and speed-ups, of minute accents and withdrawals of accents—even the attack with the bow—that characterize his cello playing.

When musicians get together to talk about him, the background sound to conversation is a constant "laeei–dugadaeei," spaciously expressed. His "laeei" is his means of communication as a conductor, just as his playing is his means of communication as a cello teacher or in chamber music.

Fortunately for this book, his facial expressions and gestures communicate, too. Musicians who have worked with him unhesitatingly translate each Valaitis photograph into a fingering instruction, or a place where the orchestra is too loud or out of tune. They know precisely what he is doing in each photo, sometimes even to a specific note in a specific piece by a particular composer. They know what sound he is making, too—"laeei" or "dugadugadaeei" — and they inevitably sing it. Their reactions to the Valaitis photographs, along with some of Casals' own observations about music and life, make up the bulk of the text of this book.

But the text is a pretext; the photographs are the real matter. One hopes that the text serves to slow the reader down so that the photographs have plenty of time to register, so that details can sink in and gain meaning—and form a design.

"Play the design, not the notes," Casals says, again and again, to the musicians that he draws to himself like a magnet.

May one suggest his exhortation to the readers of this book, too?

—*Theodore Strongin*

BIOGRAPHY

*P*ablo Casals was born in Vendrell, about forty miles from Barcelona, on December 29, 1876. His full name at birth was Pau (Catalan for Pablo) Carlos Salvador Defilló de Casals. His father was an organist in the local church and an ardent liberal.

His earliest memories are of his parents' cottage by the Mediterranean at San Salvador, where he built his own home thirty years later.

He was a natural at music. At the age of five, he sang second soprano in the local church choir. His father taught him piano and violin, and later, when he could reach the pedals, organ. At seven he could write music. At eight he sometimes played in church when his father could not be there.

His father built him his first cello with a gourd as a sounding board. This instrument is still in Casals' San Salvador home, and he can claim it if he ever chooses to end his exile.

At eleven, he went to study at the Municipal School of Music in Barcelona. His father, who objected, wanted his son to become a carpenter's apprentice. His mother took him to Barcelona, put him up with relatives, and later joined him there.

He began his rebellion against the old conventions of cello playing at Barcelona—against the stiff bow arm and restricted fingering. Meanwhile, he earned money by playing for dances in a local bar. The pianist and composer Isaac Albeniz heard him there, and sent him to the Count de Morphy, a patron of music in Madrid.

From 1894 to 1897, Casals lived in Madrid with his mother and two younger brothers under the count's patronage and that of Queen Cristina, to whom the count had introduced him. Meanwhile, Casals studied at the Royal Conservatory. He became personally attached to the Spanish royal family, but his personal relationships never influenced his political judgment of them.

The count wanted Casals to compose Spanish operas. His mother insisted that the cello come first. So the family went to Brussels, where Casals attended the conservatory for one day and then left it because it was "too jocular."

The Casals family, now near destitution, went to Paris. Pablo earned four francs a day at a music hall. Then they went back to Catalonia, where Casals taught at the municipal music school, played first cello at the Barcelona Opera, gave concerts and entertained at resorts until he had enough money to go back to Paris. He was twenty-two. Leaving some money with his family, he went on alone. Count de Morphy gave him an introduction to the conductor Charles Lamoureux. He made his debut as a soloist in a concert directed by Lamoureux on Nov. 12, 1899.

At this time he began playing the Bach unaccompanied suites for cello in public. He had been studying them privately for twelve years.

He had no trouble finding engagements after his Paris debut. He toured throughout Europe and the Americas, including the United States. He even got to see the wild West. In later years, westerns were to be among his favorite television fare.

He gave many performances with the violinist Jacques Thibaud and the pianist Alfred Cortot. Among his friends were Ravel, Saint-Saens, and Fritz Kreisler, and outside the world of music, Henri Bergson, Léon Blum, and Georges Clemenceau.

After World War I, Casals founded the Pau Casals Orchestra in Barcelona, subsidizing it for several years with a total worth about $320,000 at that time, before it became self-supporting. Casals considers orchestras "the greatest of all instruments." Conducting has meaning for him.

During the 1920's, Casals developed the Workingmen's Concert Association. For six pesetas a year, its members attended performances of the Pau Casals Orchestra and formed their own groups. He also continued to tour internationally and was guest conductor of such orchestras as the London Symphony, the New York Symphony, and the Vienna Philharmonic.

Casals always had humanistic political convictions. He did not object to the overthrow of the old regime in Russia, but he refused to perform there after 1917 because of his feeling about the inhumanities of the new regime. He protested against Nazi Germany and Fascist Italy in the 1930's. In 1936, he came out on the Republican side of the Spanish Civil War, against Franco, performing benefit concerts for the victims of Franco's men. He rejected overtures from the Monarchists, saying he "would not be a party to either a republic or a monarchy, but would accept the regime freely chosen by my own country."

During a 1938 international radio broadcast of one of his Barcelona concerts, he pleaded, "do not commit the crime of letting the Spanish Republic be murdered. If you allow Hitler to win in Spain, you will be the next victims of his madness. The war will spread to all Europe, to the whole world. Come to the aid of our people." He spoke first in English, then in French.

When Franco's victory loomed, in 1939, Casals went into voluntary exile, saying that he would not return until the Spanish people had a government of their own choice.

Soon after his exile, he settled in Prades, a town in the French Pyrenees in which many Catalan refugees had gathered. He remained in France during World War II to help his fellow exiles.

He began touring again after World War II, but while in England in the fall of 1945 it became clear to him that the democratic nations were not going to withdraw their support of Franco. He cut his tour short, played a few benefits (the last in 1947) and refused to accept any invitation to play or conduct. His audiences were his pupils and friends in his home at Prades.

Since Casals would not go to them, prominent musicians began to come to him. Alexander Schneider led a contingent to Prades in 1950 and convinced Casals to take part in what turned out to be a long line of Prades festivals. The first was in honor of the 200th anniversary of the death of Bach.

On January 28, 1956, Casals made his first concert appearance in nine years outside Prades. It was at Veracruz, Mexico. During the trip he visited Puerto Rico, where his mother was born. He stayed there three months and later that year returned to settle. In 1957, the first annual Festival Casals was held in Puerto Rico, with the help of Alexander Schneider and the Puerto Rican government.

In 1958, he gave a cello recital at the United Nations in New York. In 1961, he played at the White House for President Kennedy. His last visit to the White House had been in 1902, for Theodore Roosevelt.

In 1962, he conducted his own oratorio, *El Pesebre,* in Carnegie Hall. In 1963, he brought Bach's *St. Matthew Passion* from Puerto Rico to New York, and in 1964, Haydn's *The Creation.*

Since 1961 Casals has been going to the Marlboro [Vermont] School and Festival for a few weeks each summer to teach master classes and conduct the chamber orchestra. He is among old friends there. Rudolf Serkin, the pianist, is artistic director and Alexander Schneider attends regularly. So do many of the younger people who make up Casals' festival orchestra in Puerto Rico.

Casals still plays and conducts at Prades in the summer, going there after Marlboro. By now, Soviet artists have joined the Prades entourage. Casals also has other European summer commitments now, Bachian, festival-like ones. But he returns to Puerto Rico each fall. He does not like cold weather.

The Casals home in Puerto Rico overlooks the sea. It is located on the outskirts of San Juan.

Casals will be ninety years old on December 29, 1966. His daily routine has changed little in many years. He begins his day at seven o'clock with a solitary walk for one hour. "On my return I sit at the piano. I play Bach, to give the house the necessary atmosphere."

In August 1957, Casals married Martita Montanez, a cello student of his, sixty years younger than he. His first two marriages, to the Portuguese cellist, Guilhermina Suggia (1906), and the American singer, Susan Metcalfe (1914), ended in divorce. There are no children.

puerto rico

*P*ablo Casals' mother came from a Catalan family that had emigrated to Puerto Rico. She was born there and lived there until she was eighteen, when she came to Spain.

In 1956, at the age of seventy-nine, Casals arrived for his first visit, accompanied by a pupil, Martita Montanez, eighteen, the daughter of a well-known family of musicians in Puerto Rico.

"I recognized the countryside, the sea that Mother had so often described to me. She never returned to Puerto Rico, but she was often nostalgic for it."

Late in 1956, Casals came to Puerto Rico for good.

*C*asals lives in a white ranch house with a red tile roof, modest in size, on the edge of the sea near San Juan.

His mother's maiden name was Defillo. Many of the Defillos in Puerto Rico claim relationship with him, which delights him. "I have more than fifty relatives in the Antilles, between Puerto Rico, Cuba, and Santo Domingo."

"One of the first words that I heard from my mother was 'Puerto Rico.' She always remembered her island, so far from her. It became a dream that lasted all my life. It is a dream that I am sorry that I came to realize only in my advanced age."

"I feel that Puerto Rico is mine. The sea, the small towns — a beautiful thing, very small. The landscape is the one I thought of all my life, because my mother used to describe it to me."

"Isn't that shirt typical! He always wears one like it and the bottom button is always unbuttoned."

Joseph Haydn
Die Schöpfung
Oratorium

Verlag von
BREITKOPF & HÄRTEL
in
LEIPZIG

Nr. 680

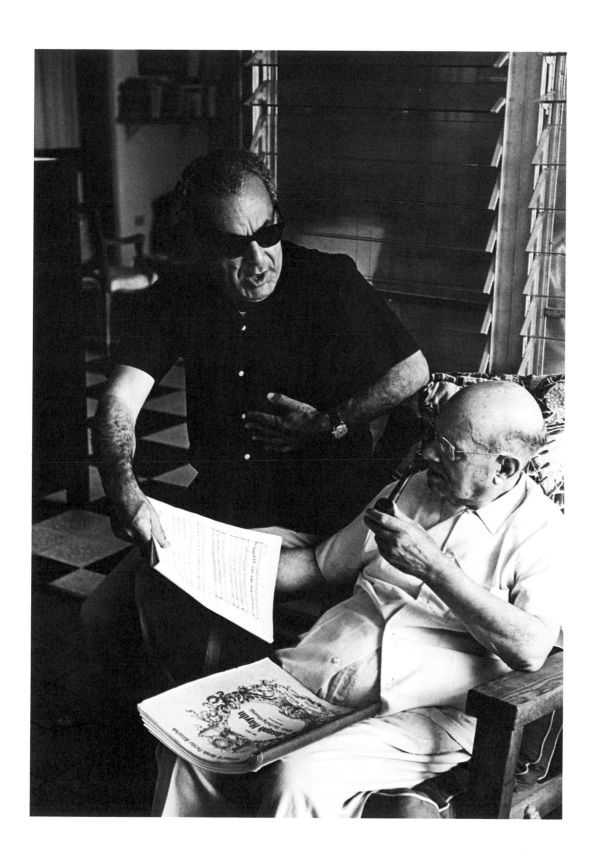

"What I think is that sensibility has been lost today, so many things have happened in the world lately. Today we see fantastic things in science, in everything; in machines that do a lot of things.

"I will say only elemental things—nothing complex—as everything ought to be, beginning with life. But you must know that the simplest things are the ones that count.

"But the world has forgotten sadly the most elemental things. What I feel very deeply is that the world has retrogressed, gone back in many ways, and especially in sensibility. I remember, for instance, the time of the Dreyfus case. It was only one man, and everyone—everyone! —at that time was interested in this case. If an injustice was committed to one man, everyone questioned it.

"Today we forget the millions of lives lost in the last wars. We rather tend to think of other things that refer to our physical needs, to our amusements. That is why I think that the world is going backwards.

"We have more and more people that think they know everything there is to be known, except Pater Noster."

A couple of boys were leaning on the fence in City Hall Park
in Manhattan, listening to the Casals Festival Orchestra, fresh from
Puerto Rico, playing a concert from the steps.

"Once in a while it's good to hear sweet music. You know what
I mean; when you got nothing else to do."

"Yeah. . . . That Casals, they say he's ninety-nine years old."

"That's nothing. My grandfather is a hundred and twenty."

"I know no one who doesn't think of him as a symbol of musical integrity. He is so completely musical. Every sound he draws, every motion of his left hand, is for musical means, rather than instrumental ones."

"Playing under him is more like playing chamber music than being in an orchestra. There's much more individual involvement."

"He's not really a conductor, but that doesn't matter. He transmits what he wants to the orchestra."

"For me, one of the high points was the *St. Matthew Passion* in Puerto Rico. We had all the time we needed to work on it. It was a stupendous personal project, a revelation, as if Casals really embraced the *St. Matthew* and made it a kind of personal message. Everything he takes hold of has a kind of personal, fervent stamp. Every note he plays or conducts or sings is the most important in the world at that time."

"There's something deceptively simple about him. He won't be pinned down to anything specific. Someone once asked him to explain why he wanted such a high F-sharp. All he said was—he was scowling—"It's flat, it's flat, it's too low. You should know this before you come to me."

"My God, I'm scared again already. He looks so stern. That's such a typical expression."

"But that look is a mask. You don't really know what's going on."

"You know what I notice of these pictures? They're so many of them very stern. I don't see many of him smiling."

"He doesn't really express happiness or joy much when he rehearses."

"Maybe, but when his face lights up, it's like an angel. It's beautiful."

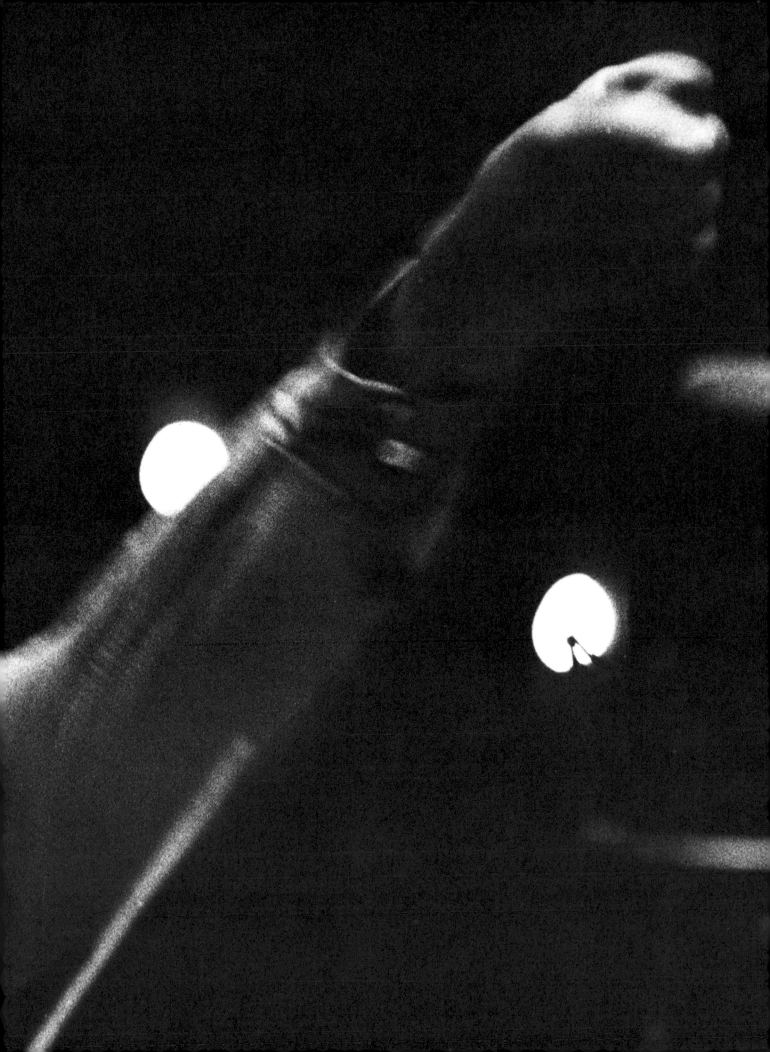

"I have always, when I go out on stage to play, a pain here, in the chest. All my life it's been like that. It's worst of all when I am playing solo. When I play a duet with a pianist, there's less pain and still less when I play with a chamber group.

"Best of all for me is when I don't play at all, but conduct."

"There's a smile. 'Lo-o-ovely, Lo-o-ovely,' he's saying."

"Those who have known him longest agree affectionately that he is no plaster saint. He was probably born ambitious, selfish and not a little acquisitive. He has always known his own value, and like any good Catalan, still knows what is good or bad business. The organization of the festivals leaves no doubt on that score, and his flow of pupils—some of them rich— supplies him with a deserved income.

"His life . . . is frugal, but not austere and certainly never lonely. There is a constant stream of visitors and admirers from all over the world, as well as a devoted circle of friends and family, several of whom go and come freely from his charming seaside villa. . . ."

"A little rosy apple of a robust countryman, he could easily pass as an English vicar on his summer holiday, with his panama hat, gold spectacles and well-laundered but shapeless tussore shirt and a Sherlock Holmes pipe curling out of his mouth."

Once, when asked how much he smokes, he replied, "As much as possible."

"Martita's tuning the cello for him. It's not that he can't turn the pegs. He's got strong arms. Remember the time in Puerto Rico, when the performance ended? He wanted Sascha to get up. He wanted the orchestra to stand immediately. Sascha wouldn't do it. I guess Sascha was pleased but he wanted Casals to get the applause. It was one of those few times that Sascha wouldn't really do what Casals asked, especially on stage. Casals grabbed Sascha's arm and yanked him out of the chair.

"Somebody's got to tune it. He won't. You know what he does? When there's a friend or a student in the room, Casals sits with the cello and one of them will turn the pegs while he uses the bow.

"You turn the peg, usually the D string. The pegs are usually very stiff from the Puerto Rican humidity. He has his pipe in his mouth. He grunts 'Arragh'—that means higher. Or 'Urragh'—that's lower.

"One of the things he gets angry at us all for is not displaying enough commitment. 'Why are you afraid to express yourselves? Bad taste is better than none at all.' He is surprised when a young player gets up and fails to communicate himself."

"He loves the old corn—variations on *The Daughter of the Regiment*—all those. Some of the dyed-in-the-wool twentieth-century musicians have no particular regard for Casals. They disagree exactly with this personal involvement. Stravinsky once said something like, 'Casals is merely content to play Bach in the style of Brahms all his life.'"

*l*ed by Sascha Schneider, the cream of today's musicians have come to Puerto Rico. Rudolf Serkin has been there. So have Artur Rubinstein and Yehudi Menuhin. Among the younger ones, the Guarneri String Quartet describes itself as "Really a septet. The four of us, plus Sascha, Rudy [Serkin] and Casals."

Governor Luis Muñoz Marin of Puerto Rico has encouraged the festivals as a way of counteracting the effects of "Operation Bootstrap"—industrialization. The festivals have helped rejuvenate Puerto Rico's cultural life, just as Casals' activities did for Catalonia in the 1920's. Muñoz Marin is grateful.

But Muñoz Marin, himself a poet, is not just political about Casals; he is emotional. He once wanted to have Casals' name strung up in lights in a great electric display in San Juan, a traditional honor for historical figures. An official objected: "But Don Pablo is still alive." Muñoz Marin answered, "Don't you know the difference between someone simply alive and an immortal?"

marlboro etc.

*M*arlboro is a village in Vermont about six miles west of Brattleboro. In the summer, Rudolf Serkin directs (or shares, as he insists) a music school and festival there.

"It was inevitable that Casals should come to Marlboro. So many of the older ones there had been his associates and colleagues, headed by Rudy and Sascha, of course."

Casals conducts the Marlboro orchestra and holds master classes there for a few weeks each summer.

Things elsewhere

Tonight, July 12,
at 7:15 p.m.

Orchestra Rehearsal
(Mozart symph.
#39)

"There is nothing of a show here. Everything is as natural and simple as this feeling that we are here present as a lovely family.

"I hope that you will hear me and that something interesting will add to your knowledge.

"Variety is a great word in music, as in everything. Variety is a law—a law of nature. Look at the sea, the sky, trees, flowers. A single tree, what a miracle it is! What a fantastic creation this world is, with such diversity! That is the law of nature—diversity! That is why I can never play the same work exactly the same way twice, that is why each note, even, is a different world.

"Variety is a law, but variety with good taste, with intelligence, with intuition. I have heard hundreds of cellists, of violinists, of pianists, and they are wonderful. And after, I said, 'How annoying!' Because there is no coloring.

"Color! Color! Bach was the greatest colorist. He loved color. Beginning with the first prelude of *The Well-tempered Clavier,* only arpeggios, but what color! Color! Color! Oh! Beautiful!

"Technique, wonderful sound, all of this is something, or generally astonishing. But not enough.

"Color!

"My wife says to me, 'You are so excited all the time.' I say, 'I have to be excited; how can I help it?' "

"You know what Sascha once did? He had some beautiful publicity pictures made up for Casals. And for one of them, as a joke, he was caught with his pants off. He had everything else on. He had his shorts and his tailcoat.

"Sascha said, *'Maitre,* now which one of these publicity photos do you want?' (He had the bottom covered up). Then Sascha took his hand off. Casals turned beet red with delight. Remember? It was on stage. He broke up."

"You know, when he looked at the bust the first time, he didn't recognize it. It was embarrassing. "Lo-o-ovely, lo-o-ovely," he said. I can't remember who he thought it was. Somebody out of Mahler's time, I think."

"Casals, by his example and his nature, reminded us of something we had forgotten, or hadn't dared contemplate: the importance in music of color and variety, of feeling, warmth, involvement—in other words of ultimate human values and meaning. This man really commits himself, which is why he affects us so."

"Many of Casals' disciples mistake him when they take his emphasis on feeling, intuition, and freedom to mean a lack of discipline. There's no self-indulgence in his approach to music. 'Honesty to the limit' has been his lifelong motto, both as man and as musician.

"He himself is stubbornly disciplined. He has worked painstakingly through the most minute details of technique and conception, and it is because he has done so that in the end the details become less important than the grand design. His a discipline in the service of a liberation—that's the crucial thing.

"He has enabled us to realize that a musician can play in a way that is honest, beautiful, masculine, gently, fierce, and tender— all these together, and with unequivocal respect for the music being played, and faith in it."

"I remember playing on the Brahms sextet with him, the B-flat. The cello opens the last movement alone. I was nervous, knowing that Casals doesn't give a clear lead-in for the movement. Sascha had advised me in New York before coming down to memorize the first ten or twelve bars so that I wouldn't have to look at the music at all and I could watch Casals. And so I did memorize it—it's just a lot of noodles against his melody.

"Sure enough, he just sat there and thought for a moment or two. My heart was beating like a racehorse. I just sat there and sat there, watching. Then he suddenly took the bow and began. Of course there was no lead-in beat at all. That was a nervous moment. If I hadn't been watching . . ."

Casals is so full of life and so alert it often seems surprising that he has no use for contemporary music. He said once to a friend, "Sascha Schneider hears these modern pieces as beautiful. You hear them as beautiful. You are fine musicians, and if you hear it, there must be something there. All I cay say is that I don't hear it. I don't hear any music there."

"That's so typical. He always sits back in that easy chair as if he were born there. That shot is typical of Rudy, too."

"For me, personally, his biggest influence was not through his conducting or master classes, but through live performances and through the Bach *Unaccompanied Cello Suites.* I'll never forget the first time I heard his recording of them."

"His revelations on Bach to all us string players was one of the great events. As Sascha said, every violinist should be ashamed that it took a cellist to show the greatness of Bach's music and make it live for all of us."

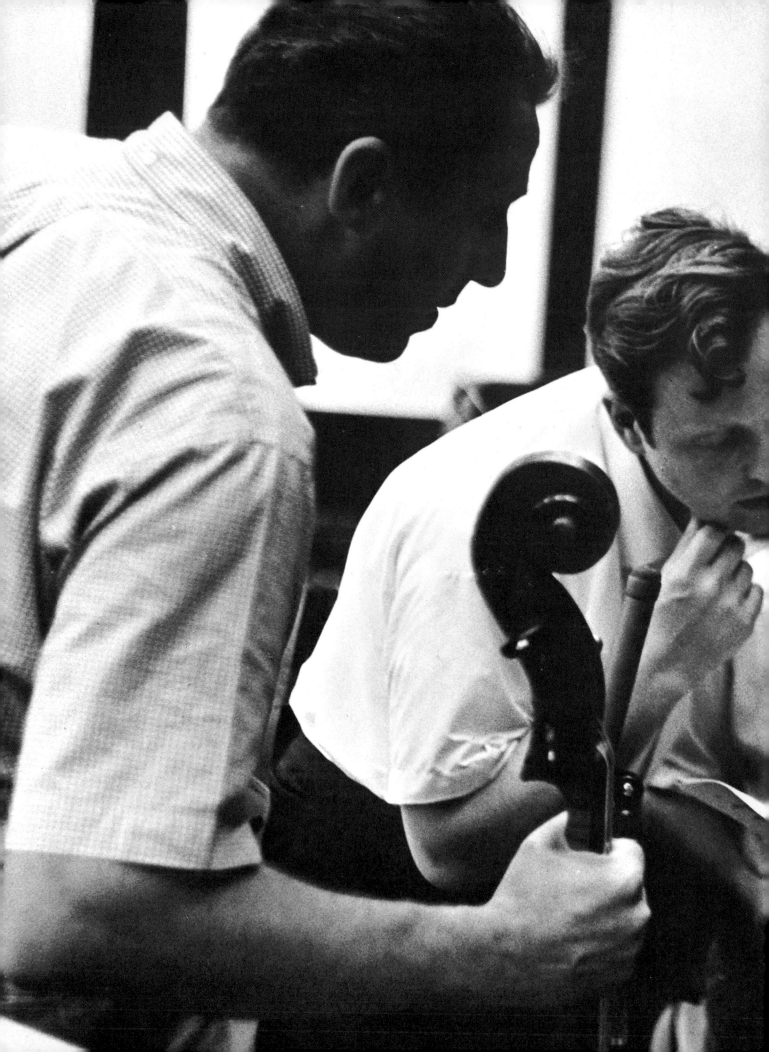

*W*hen Franco came to power, Casals said that he would never play in public again until he could play in Barcelona and he would not do that while Franco was there.

But then he came to Prades, and in 1950 Alexander Schneider convinced him to play on the Bach anniversary. His first appearance outside Prades was in Veracruz, Mexico, in 1956.

In 1958, he consented to play in the United States, but specifically at the United Nations in New York. Here is a statement he made to the press on that occasion:

i consider it an honor to have been invited by the United Nations to take part in its anniversary celebrations, and I am grateful for this opportunity to address the people of the world on a subject that preoccupies each one of us.

If at my age I have come here for this day, it is not because anything has changed in my moral attitude or in the restrictions that I have imposed upon myself and my career as an artist for all these years, but because today all else becomes secondary in comparison to the great and perhaps mortal danger threatening all humanity. Never has the world been nearer to catastrophe than at this moment. The extraordinary scientific discoveries of our century, which some great intellects, in their thirst for knowledge, have achieved, are now being exploited for the construction of instruments of monstrous destructiveness. Confusion and fear have invaded the whole world; misunderstood nationalism, fanticism, political dogmas and lack of liberty and justice are feeding mistrust and hostility that make the collective danger greater every day; yet the desire for peace is felt by every human being in the world. This desire has been manifested again and again in the face of the peril menacing all of us, by many distinguished personalities, in scientific writings, in the world press, and above all by that great citizen of the world, Dr. Albert Schweitzer.

The anguish of the world caused by the continuation of nuclear danger is increasing every day; all realize the horrifying consequences of a nuclear war, which would cause not only irreparable material and physical destruction, but also moral and spiritual degradation. How I wish that there could be a tremendous movement of protest in all countries, and especially from the mothers, that would impress those who have the power to prevent this catastrophe.

All nuclear experiments ought to be stopped altogether, and I profoundly hope that the negotiations in the near future will end in an agreement that will make this possible; only later, when calm and confidence have been re-established, then the work of the scientists could be taken up again, but only under such conditions as would benefit humanity.

In order to resolve their problems, the conflicting forces must regard as the basis for their discussions, the inhumanity and uselessness of war that all people condemn. The biggest and most powerful nations have the greater duty and responsibility for keeping peace.

It is my deep conviction that the great masses in these countries, as in every other country, want the understanding and mutual co-operation of their fellow men. It is for the governments and those in power to see to it that the achievement of this desire will not become impossible and thus cause the terrible frustration felt by all those who are not living in unconsciousness.

It seems to me that all those who believe in the dignity of man should act at this time in order to bring about a deeper understanding among peoples and a sincere *rapprochement* between conflicting forces. The United Nations today represents the most important hope for peace. Let us give it all power to act for our benefit.

And let us fervently pray that the near future will disperse the clouds that darken our days now. Music, this marvelous universal language understood by everyone everywhere, ought to be a source of better communication among men. This is why I make a special appeal to my fellow musicians everywhere, asking each one to put the purity of his art at the service of mankind in bringing about fraternal and enlightened relationships between men the world over.

The "Hymn to Joy" of Beethoven's Ninth Symphony has become a symbol of love. And I propose that every town which has an orchestra and chorus should perform it on the same day, and have it transmitted by radio to the smallest communities and to all corners of the world; and to perform it as another prayer through music for the Peace that we all desire and wait for.

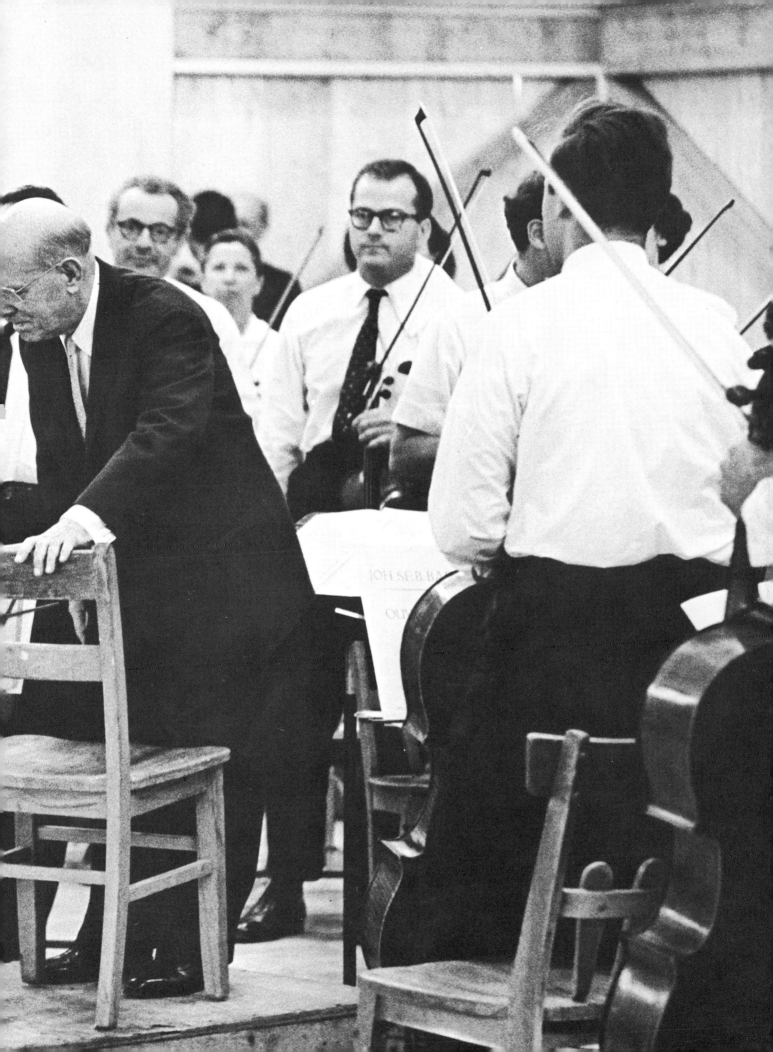

"There's a lot of embracing at Marlboro.
Here's Casals and Rudy saying farewell.
Either for the day,
or maybe just for lunch period,
or maybe Rudy's just going to the bathroom."

"This is after rehearsal, with the scarf, and they're talking about
what's going to happen tomorrow, what time the rehearsal will be. Or maybe he's
saying no rehearsal because 'Hazel' is on. That's his favorite TV show."

"Martita fiercely protects him. She is very careful about his appointments and she doesn't let him overextend himself. With his enthusiasm, he would take on too much.

"After rehearsal, she very often wipes his head off with a towel, or massages his neck.

"She learned Catalan. Do you know that he said, once, 'If I couldn't speak Catalan with my wife, I wouldn't feel I was really married.'

"I also heard him say, 'As long as you are able to admire and to love, you are young.'"

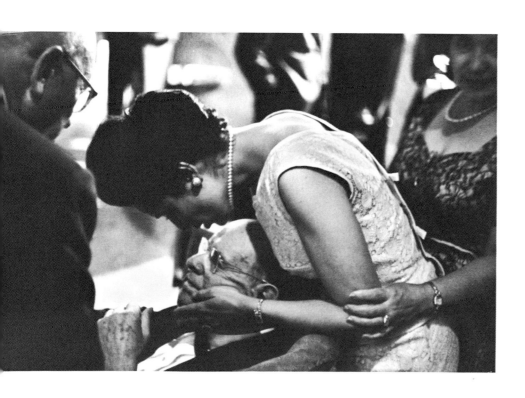